Downstate

DAVID GARDINER

David Gardiner
5 June 2009

salmonpoetry

Published in 2009 by
Salmon Poetry,
Cliffs of Moher, County Clare, Ireland
Website: www.salmonpoetry.com
Email: info@salmonpoetry.com

Paperback ISBN 978-0-9561287-3-7
(Also available in Hardback, ISBN 978-1-907056-00-0)

Cover artwork: *Sunday Bliss*, oil on canvas 76x110 cm by SERGEY TALICHKIN
www.sergeytalichkin.com
Typesetting: Patrick Chapman

"...some must watch, while some must sleep;
Thus runs the world away."

For Paula and Theo

Brick dragons luxuriate on rooftops
sleepily eyeing our descent past guttural
pigeons towards the mouth of North & Clybourn Ave.

Virgil in a cyclone cage benedicts:
the walkway; passing lights--this southbound all-stop train;
washed-out faces; snow stuck to the tracks.

They all wend down. Dispatched by morning
shadows—dim orange lauds over the Latino's shoulder.
Dragons take flight into the disappearing sky.

Acknowledgements

"Christe, Te Adoramus," *The SHOp* (Ireland), Winter 2007. "Wild Flowers" and "Bus Brakes and Debussy," *Three Candles Journal* 2007. "Plains Storm: Omaha" and "Our Best Lives," *Poetry Ireland Review 83* (Summer 2005). "Apeliotes," *The SHOp* (Fall 2005). "Blinds Down; Middle of Nowhere," *Natural Bridge: A Journal of Contemporary Literature Special Contemporary Irish Issue 7* (Spring 2002). "Patio Matins, Wisteria Court" *River King* (Illinois Arts Council) Summer 2000. "Union Station: Hausmusik," "Asleep in the city," "The C. T. A. Office: Aeolian Train," and "Four Stanzas" *Café Absinthe* Spring 2000. "Our Lady of Hibbing" *Sou'wester* Fall 1999. "The Lincoln Trail," "Militant Piety," "Heartland" *Patchwork: Images of Illinois 12* (1999). "Cartographers," and "10 O'Clock News: Pastoral," *Strong Coffee* (August and October 1998). "A Letter to Florence," *The Café Review* 8 (Spring 1997) 26. "Bungalow Belt," *Hammers* 12 (Winter 1997) 54. "Nobody Move and Nobody Gets Hurt," "Border Ballad," *OYEZ Review* 24 (1996) 79-80. "Trepidations," *Apostrophe* 1.2 (Fall/Winter 1996) 59. "The August Restoration," *Hyphen* 12 (Fall 1996) 65. "Damned Crickets," *Mostly Maine* 17 (1996) 44. "Four Stanzas," "Apeliotes," *Chants* (Spring 1996). "Bride of the Wind: Queen of Gretna, NE." *Tomorrow Magazine* 15 (Spring 1996) 10. "Ode to Buzzy Santos." *American Goat* 6 (Spring 1995) 11-12.

Cover photo: © Chicago Tribune photographer John Smierciak. Tom Skilling writes "on assignment southwest of Peoria on Rt. 136 near Havana, Ill., [Smierciak] captured cold frontal storm clouds as dozens of twisters raked sections of 6 states, including downstate Illinois and Indiana. NOAA's Storm Prediction Center tallied 37 reports of twisters in that day's severe weather outbreak."

Contents

III. The Heartlands

I. Backstreets & indifferent stars

"There's no true season for salvation here. Good times or hard, it's still an infidel's capital six days a week.

And with a driving vigor and a reckless energy unmatched in the memory of man. Where only yesterday the pungent odor of stewed dog trailed across the marshes, now the million-candled billboards, weaving drunken lights in the river's depths, boast of Old Fitzgerald, Vat 69, White Horse, and Four Roses. Where only yesterday evening the crow crossed only the lonely teepee fires, now the slender arc-lamp burns.

To reveal our backstreets to the indifferent stars."

— Nelson Algren, *City on the Make*

Nobody Move and Nobody Gets Hurt

"Nobody move and nobody gets hurt."
Imperfect iambic pentameter
Echoes through the velvet-roped public space,
forces us to face our flat-speaking ground.

I can hear the boiler-room—still the heart-
beat of all this glass and steel. Still that heart
and you can feel the iamb in your veins,
moving like two Polish aunts through one revolving door...

Moving like a long letter to Baldoyle,
like big Lithuanians dancing in Grant Park,
like an old A-train through a B station.

Stuck still waving over the tellers' plaques,
Audrey C., Louise L., and Thomas E.
seem to be in little danger. Being

a nobody, I watch the iambs move.

Pigeon Grace

Taxis move like water bugs on L.S.D.
I've been waking to slow doves on the three-flat,
streetlights, and full moons in the morning sky.

Another black and blue pigeon hangs,
indifferent and alone in the updraft
as the northbound subway becomes the EL.

I can't help but cross myself at mid-day
at a procession of cabs with lights on;
we have missed so many ways out of here.

We've been saved, not chosen—
standing in September puddles;
city birds who can't shake loose their own oils.

A feather pulled from your pillow
falls into the sun square on the wood floor,
lands in that short time of grace--

echoes that same silence, as the train doors open, and
I've forgotten the day and my stop.

Union Station, Hausmusik

The Rail Club serves its specials in styrofoam
Hung out like mail for the straight-railed ride home.
The vast majority of this small and undistinguished
    group tip
Rarely—their hands, or money—to a bartender
Who learned to speak english twenty-seven years ago
From <u>Old Mr. Boston's De Luxe Bartending Guide</u>.

Sixty-three some odd feet above the bar lean three statues:
Justice without her scales; Astrea with a blackbird; and
Andromache without wings. Each of the draped and
    dusty women butt their
Heads on the ceiling barely missing the gray and moving
Cameras—plastic shaded balls on a tin and gothic ceiling.

Only Andromache seems disturbed by the anachronism.
But she likes Chicago too well, thinks the station's
    "fascinating"
And the "hustle and bustle" somewhat "exciting."
The globes float like lint in a laundromat, out of Astrea's way
And far beyond Justicia's considerations, sword, or flail.

By the next time around, we're actually hoping these cameras
Will be mirrored. These gray worlds will finally move us
    all to dance,
And, as promised, each and every evening in the privacy of
    our own homes
We'll watch our husbands on t.v. as they finger twelve-ounce
    lidless cups,
Take account of their watches, and listen somewhat distractedly
To the next to last train move slowly out to the suburbs.

The Damned Crickets

Black case set neatly on the ground,
legs spread, back squarely to the post,
artfully long-haired, intent,
not quite timing the scream
of the tunnels & the tracks & crazy wheezing
of some other kid contorting like a ghost
to the accompaniment of a violin, and lights
blinking out--the dance of St. Vitus
on this afternoon of St. Joseph doesn't mesh.
These line-fouled reflections form a sort of
Byzantine frieze on the glass grinding through this
    Brooklyn tunnel.

The violin's hardly decipherable.
The artiste bows out the closing doors.
The front set clip that other kid a good one.

The music and dancing recede on the last platform
as I see the spitting-image of the Holy Father
in a tan fedora drop a bluesy dollar
and damn Vivaldi's crickets, *adagio*.

Border Ballad

Polish façades and Spanish billboards watch
over the piazza at Milwaukee,
Ashland, and Division Ave. The names are etched
in cement but the *rostros* change monthly.

Stanislas Saturnine emigrated here
to the near west side in 1930,
lived in the back workshop of a three-flat
and learned quickly to hammer on the pipes.
Hammered 'round the town, and jovially
made his place at funerals and weddings
playing Krakow steel drums with bare feet.
Flyers praised his "bohemian brilliance."

Capitalizing on the lack of coast-
line and vision, Stash played forgotten songs,
saved money, and earned, by investment
and violent means, his name etched deep,
today collecting exhaust, going grey
behind the *Always Open* sign of the Currency Exchange.

Apeliotes

the south-east wind, carried fruits of many kinds, wore
boots, and was not so lightly clad as the last mentioned.
—Murray's Manual of Mythology (1882)

The persistent line of ants is gone.
The fica's leaves are falling.

We'll make adjustments for the dark storm
windows, rain-marked bar-b-que, and trays
of finally dead pink impatiens on the back porch.

In time, I will walk this fallen world to the back alley,
line up the garbage in proper order,
and turn my back on all I haven't done.

In a dream I dream that Apeliotes'
winds make a new tropic—form to my wish;
seasonal decorations whirl the brown

marigolds, yellowed day-lilies away.
There the common bed of dormant bulbs rise
and are strung: ripe twinkling garland around
what I've grown to call my world.

Then, all the three-syllable months behave,
the harbingers of inactivity
will silence themselves, send us to sleep and
stumble alone down red brick gangways.

Bungalow Belt

I was born, raised in Brute, Oblivion.
Forehead squarely between shoulders
And eyes on the Eisenhower's gray pavement
Which has catapulted me across soy fields
And county lines, down lakeshores and railways,
Into the state that only distance holds.

I come from a neighborhood where "regular"
Was the supreme compliment, where my west side is
Actually called "the brickyard," and the most amazing thing
Was the Mars' factory front lawn, where a soft chocolate smell rose
From the only good-smelling plant our families knew, and where
The fat back tire of your banana seat bike was rumored to explode
If you cut the least of a line through those corners.

Whether the clay or the people came first here, I don't know.
Bricks were wrenched out of the quarry, I think,
Already colored red and holed and ready to stack
Up bungalows down the gridded gentile streets—
Short, square, solid homes; short, square, solid streets—

A stackable foundation as easily lost as the imprint on a cinder block,
The address on the curb, or a shallow handprint in a cracked sidewalk.

Stormwatch

It snows loudly here. The weather radar
provides sound effects for each sweeping arm
illustrating the revolutions and where
lightning would have struck if this had been real,
if anything was happening outside the rattling windows.

"Peace is but a pretense." Snow plows slap orange light
against the drawn white venetian blinds, toss salt against
the windshields, and run the snow off the street onto the curb
until the wide gray drifts sandbag both sides of the street.
At this hour the city sleeps in quiet white and comforting gray.

"It is a blessing of nature, that habit dulls the senses,"
I heard a plowing Montaigne mumble. At the far end of a court,
four inches deep in snow, staring dumbly at the hoop, I know
no more cement feeling than this; waiting for the streetlights
to go off and the pick ups to return--dingoes to cold carcasses.

Asleep in the city

Asleep in the city
rattling afternoon trucks
Zephyr & Debussy on WNIB
or a scratchy Coltrane tape to
roll through your shadowed nursery.

Upstairs our neighbor seems to be listening
to top 40 radio for the fiftieth time today.

I look around for where you get your peace.
I can't remember sleeping through one of these afternoons...

I turn down the radio and envy
your peach comforter, your pacifier,
all those oxymoronic things
(except maybe the vaporizer)
that sound as out of place as urban living.

My Baby Bathed in Neon Light

My baby bathed in neon light,
Sleepless, staring for the dark through the night.

At midnight on a still, too warm late March,
I'm looking for something else to tell you,
Notice in the black & white of Ashland Playlot
That the shadowed buds have gone to flower
Before I had noticed a single leaf.

In the gray of an open loading dock,
I trace black branches on magenta skies,
Pray to the white-green moon of St. Alphonsus's clock,
Drift off to the sound of the torn chain net
Brushing the iron of the white steel backboard.

My baby bathed in neon light,
Sleeping, redeeming the dark through the night.

Third Shift

Above the refrigerator's hum
and neighbor's footsteps on my head,
I can hear my daughter stretch,
my dogs fidget, and my wife sleep.

Friday night traffic hasn't stopped,
the screens are still propped in the windows
and open our front room to bar close,
Hostess truck deliveries and 3 a.m.
grocery carts taking cans up the uneven sidewalk.

The neighbor always passes out eventually.
The light of his t.v. going blue on the brick wall.
Shopping carts in the same alley will disappear in gray light,
and at some point the humming light above the sink
will give way slowly to the more normal sounds—

the same cars not starting,
newspaper machines slamming shut,
and both of you shuffling across cold floors
knowing nothing much has happened again.

Imaginary Mazurkas

Diversy and Mobile St.

At night, I look for the big-kettled kitchens. Turn full from
    the parkway,
stare through windows, and try to lift a view from the gone
    beat cop.

Through a broken blind, I see the women running the home,
catch glimpses of their mute dresses passing open bedrooms,
casting shadows across the front hallway.

Dzia dzias sit in red-orange lumpy chairs, unread newspapers folded,
antimacassars crumpled everywhere.

These shadows box tonight with the radiator hiss of wind
    through dead elms,
the sound of truck breaks on the tollway overhead.

Sophie will wake up at four and cook dinner for Chrissy to warm.
Len will come home laughing and sleepy, toss a heavy lunch box
    on the table.
Adam and his granddaughter will fall asleep watching Gorgeous George.

The whole picture fades in miniature as I squint past my collar.
Windows steam and blue light creeps out. Through snowflakes
    the size of mothballs
The metal blinds are giving way back to those same lace curtains.
Turning the corner, I see the snow and petals of glass down
    the alley—
a sparkling, broken river of milk bottles from a tomorrow morning

that has yet to happen again. It reaches west beyond Harlem
    Avenue,
away from this small square of light and rattle of the past.

Bus brakes and Debussy

Our loves wing out—
Heavy planes
Over Rikers.

Saturday morning traffic a low tide,
silver cranes stretch the sky past Harlem.
Air brakes & busses wash under Sloan-Kettering,
gears downshifting up York Ave.

Our loves wing out—
Heavy planes
Over Rikers.

We lie and listen to a city
out of tune—aeolian tunnels, screeching bridges.
Every taxi's caught curb is a sore finger
on the wrong string.

Our loves wing out—
Heavy planes
Over Rikers.

I watch my wishes on the backs of planes
above these noises. The remote speaker is warm &
a little bigger than your hand,
quiet, balanced too often on this bedrail.

Entomology: Natural History Museum, Dublin

for Steffani

Italian, Polish & silly laughter at tit birds
fill the dead zoo. I head straight by
kits perpetually at play back to the hawk moths.

Pink & green & ridiculous, they're mounted under glass.
I think of them hovering around foxgloves,
scolding me for drinking their nectar out of fuchsia.

Looking for that iridescent green moth again,
I realize I know nothing about them. Noctuidae,
hemiptera, and even *callophrys rubi* seem all the same to me...

Then I hear a couple call a mountain ringlet 'boring.'
I want to turn on them & tell them, "the last one,
the last one, was taken at Lough Gill in 1895,

that whatever their gropey, bored hands think,
this single blue-brown moth hasn't been seen in a century."
But they're gone too. I'm left with the true bugs.

Smashed capsids & a hilariously mounted leafhopper
now have me pinned here in the back of the museum.
There's nothing boring again.

By the time the kids have bought their plastic animals,
I'm leaning on the case, laughing at myself in love
with the cock-chafer's eye-lashes, rose-chafer's shell—

the delicate beauty of the tortoise beetle;
all the delineations & small wildness of a world
we hold forever in our hands.

II. Our Best Lives

We are continually living a solution to problems that reflection cannot hope to solve.

— J. H. Van den Berg

Our Best Lives

for Thomas Dillon Redshaw

We live our best lives in small dark houses
knowing the landing's last step
and the upstairs hallway's turn.

We live our best lives mowing short lawns
on the one hot Sunday in March
watching the wheels, not speaking.

We live our best lives in spite of ourselves
with Tuesday laundry forgotten
without an hour on the porch.

In spite of ourselves, the back lock that sticks,
the empty kitchen window,
and the tilted room of light in the yard,

we live our best lives.

Locking Windows

Shutting out the night, I don't want to know that
anything goes on; that when I lie down
on cold sheets a whole world could continue on
front porches, that somewhere maybe three doors
down, someone's watching my lights go off and
thinking that shutting down would be 'real nice'
just this night, maybe hoping that
the train wouldn't whistle
crossing Wood Street and that falling asleep
wouldn't mean that promising not to have
another day that ends watching
shadows change color on the wall and drapes
go from sheer to black in all the good houses.

In the backward season

for Seán Lucy

The wind is cold through the sycamores.
Snakes curl on the warming ground.

I know I can see them. Beneath dry river rocks,
wrapped around broken hickory branches;
hear them, in the hissing smoke
of leaves I forgot to burn last fall.

Woodpeckers work unseen.
We other scavengers and carrion things
hack at the edges, holding on to the scruffy heights
and riverwash till the hawks arrive.

An egret, flying low, would take little notice
of our out-of-season pecking order

would land at his own behest,
disdainful of the cold silty water,
turn his head to branches snapping,
turn again toward the bad wind from the east,

probably, like me now, wonder
when his unforgiving cousins will return
& set all this to right.

Buffalo, IL

The linoleum's curling under foot.
It feels no different than the fields outside—
dusted with snow, broken by winter,
no memory of the ground green with soy in summer.

I'm reading tea bags in the stainless drain
by a 60-watt bulb over the sink.
Watching my half hour of peace disappear
with watermarks under the dishrag.

Listening at the dark turn of the stairs,
I pray without hope to dish racks,
to half-empty laundry baskets, that color returns
fold back through this long dark and fold around me.

Our Lady of Hibbing

Grace is the patron saint of spotted deer.
Her white wings spread at night between headlights,
soar through the gray mornings over Leech Lake.

The problem is that you can't look for Grace
in this Minnesota town where we're not
tricked by thaws, quieted by August frost.

It's like we're high centered on a fire road--
solid old ruts through the iron range where
morning stars stay buried under March snow.

Grace stands in the diamond of light pitched up
between shadows of crossed blackened birch trees
and what looks to be a still, standing doe

staring into that limbo of sunrise
when the light breaks the horizon, peaks out
to disappear again under the dark

mined out and run over Mesabi Range.

Butterfield Road, Icestorm

Ice-caked trees shine like back-lit crystal
in the grocery store; a lithograph
fading from memory back into black
& white, with three stray geese in formation,
and impossibly pink cirrus clouds folding
all jet streams to a triple point.

The sound of semis & the red behind the frosted trees
go gray in the rearview mirror at 50 miles an hour.
Driving back into the extending dark,
chasing El Caminos through turns lanes as
I wait on complete night when all the ice goes clear again,
and all the foaming horses head back south.

Plains storm, Omaha

Around here, a truck's rumble past is
as natural as wind that rocks the porch swing in your absence.

"God doesn't give his thunder to us all."
We tell ourselves we're lucky; with our daylilies and dogwoods—

we're the stuff that survives, has roots and mind
enough not to stick our heads above neighboring flowers.

The winds, the sirens, and the early bathtimes
all fall together to make our long horizons,

hang together as the front porchswing rocks
with silhouettes of wild roses waiting for the storm.

The front of a life that blows in from elsewhere.

Empty Beds

The morning's cold enough to make
the sheets too warm to leave.
I dress straight out of bed,
the last to wake, long after breakfast.

One night of frost changes a season of hard work or love,
those things we confuse for each other around here.
There's a list on the kitchen counter--
"storms on house, cracked window,
quilts & comforters in attic."

Two night's frost has bent the yard to attention.
Unblackened rose buds caught in limbo
sway out under short, low sunshine.
The cherries cling near the dogwood.
The bees do their work slow, unperturbed.

I stop on the back walk alone in the cold.
Morning light just over the houses,
frost on shadowed squares of grass.
I stare dumbly at the impatiens,
four feet tall after a long summer.

The pink, whites, purples, and reds
lean against the house, bend towards the ground,
all contracting into two greens:
the dark green of the frosted leaves &
the light frozen stalks; both standing & dying by water.

They all seem to be asking me,
"Why did you forsake the kindness of even an old sheet?"
The Classifieds blew over one last night &
it seems to be holding up dirty petals, asking
as I undo that headscarf, "oh, I must look awful."

I promise to leave their beds alone.
Let them fare with what dignity the season affords.
Yet what's left is convincing me to hang on to what's gone.
And though I'll have all Indian Summer to look
at dead impatiens' empty beds, tonight they'll be covered.

Epiphany Song

for James Liddy

> *Orpheus could lead the savage race;*
> *And trees unrooted left their place,*
> *Sequacious of the lyre;*
> *But bright Cecilia rais'd the wonder higher:*
> *When to her organ vocal breath was given,*
> *An angel heard, and straight appear'd*
> *Mistaking Earth for Heaven.*
>   —John Dryden

The cold returns without the Christmas lights.
This week when the holiday ends,
I stop at my daughters' parent-appreciation mass.
No post-sixties "stand & be recognized,"
I'm alone in hangover territory in the back pews
with a good view of the manger in the
Our Lady of Nebraska Chapel.

Either the warmth, or the sleep, or the children's voices
at morning mass bring me to almost perfect prayer
Defend the cause of the poor of the people,
give deliverance to the needy…
May you all live while the sun endures,
and as long as the moon,
throughout all generations…
like rain that falls on the mown grass,
like showers that water the earth…
May righteousness flourish and peace abound,
and peace abound, until the moon is no more. (Ps. 72)

I tag my poems to all your daughters' song,
traveling up on light with Suger's angels.
With "Three Kings," I pray that twenty children,
then thought fifty, and then got greedy thinking,
why not *all* of them grow up truly good people.

And that's when I lost my daughters.

Not till after mass, catching sight of Alexis & Izzy,
did I see my oldest daughter as I nearly walked over her.
Even after she pointed out her younger sister
    laughing at me,
I barely saw her. Walking away, a head taller than the rest,
taller than I remember even this morning,
blonde hair over her backpack, gray-blue eyes glaring
at her big sister when she ran up to say, "Dad's here."

Flashing to say, "Don't embarrass me in front of Alex;
I'm grown up." I walk away,
touching the font like her forehead,
listening to the organ doodling
wondering if anyone will bring it up
when I walk in late & they're eating tonight.

Painting Grays

I have tried to emphasize that those people...have dug the earth with those very hands they put in the dish....All winter long I have had threads of this tissue in my hands, and have searched for the ultimate pattern."
—Van Gogh, 30 April 1885

Black blue crows and brown cardinals set
the palette for the gnarled hickories--
bent steel against an iron April sky.

Anything sublime wouldn't stand up here.
It'd be wiped out easier than brown
desperate leaves by the never distant

sounds of two or three interstate truck routes.
It's hard to make this place mean anything.
Even storms pick up speed running through here.

Though imagination does, our nature
does not lead west. Realizing this, we parked
in the dead center of a flat continent.

In our worst moments, even the clouds stare
vacantly at the heartland, its closed mines,
corporate farms, child brides, and dirty children.

I could paint these leafless trees again but
the sky would still be iron over peeling bark,
and I could not create a color not seen.

It would be pointless to date the canvas.
My plain people are timeless, tired, gray
and don't need another April to remind them

of the faith they've never put in the spring.
We exist like birds you never notice
who claim the gray sky with their grounded song.

Hunger Moon

I'll wander from St. Gennero
to Iowa cornfields
between the harvest and Halloween.

The last moon is out
over Lakeville, Minnesota
and I'll see it Sunday morning

watching this bedroom community
from the Municipal Liquor Store
parking lot. The good people

drink coffee from Supersaver
mugs in the cold morning.
I watch the trucks run south on I-35,

can't picture Texas, or Thunder Bay,
but thank their good God for the chance
to fill the car with Iowa ethanol

and drive my family to any home at all.

Not a love sonnet

If I love your most obvious weakness
& life's not the pursuit of pleasure,
then I seem to be set for the long haul.
But then there's kids & soccer & simple sunshine,
or this twice a week goldfish feeling
I get driving past my own two square house
looking out the windows of the CR-V, XL-7,
or whatever alphabet I'm dreaming that day.

Not until I'm back on my back with you,
busting up all these clouds in my head,
can I see the brightening gray cirrus roads
lining the sky that I think you see too

against dawn skies that I rarely wake to see.

Wild Flowers

Long, late April
in Nebraska &
I've spent the day
looking elsewhere.

Pulling azaleas away from the house,
giving them another last chance
for a season on their own
behind the garage, I grow to appreciate
all the dangers of lye, high ph in the soil,
minerals wicking off century old foundation stones.

What gives me peace,
takes their blossoms &
burns their roots,
leaves their branches brittle.

It's a sort of osteoporosis of nature.
That which shelters us
stunts the wildest flowers we have.
Even the roses will answer my daconill love
with black spot & rust
if I provide it on my own time:

In that July hour of the afternoon
between sleepy wasps &
wisteria fluff, when
Marlene & the girls have gone.

Nature demands her schedule:
water early & feed in the stillness.
The wildest blooms we have
are stunted by anything

which comes to them upon any
but their own terms.

This may be why, on the porch working out
these poems, I both love & wince at the tumble
of return, with after-school snacks & homework.
The comforting din of love flowering
on its own schedule.

The Heartland

We live among the half wild houses,
trailers sunk in concrete;
converted carports

out here among the horse people,
tight hacking groups who burn their grass.
Their white-headed colt watches me

walking the dog, starting the car,
turning the blinds of our back room
at night, against the flash of a neighbor's motion light.

We're bypassed out here on Old 51.
Trucks roar toward Memphis
trains whistle in the 3 a.m. distance.

Not a porchlight turns on these things
we're not concerned with. Everyone's
at home. In the blue-curtained light

there's little to tell us where we are;
little to tell us that we're on the margin,
little to tell us anything,

until late at night,
the last train to New Orleans past,
we hear the one,

persistent bark of a coyote,
and roll again into unremembered dreams.

Small Plane to Memphis

Wanda's drawl is so beautiful—
       "born and raised in Memphis, hon…"
That I wouldn't mind if she told me
       "we're all going down now."

Even over the drone of the props,
       the safety instructions sound like
Gillian Welch singing,
       "Down to the river to pray…"

Everything lately sounds like that to me,
       though I'm not anxious to be saved,
Or to meet anybody's maker.
       I'm at peace bouncing back over *Missoura*.

Looking down on the farms beyond
       Springfield, I'm thinking
I can pray & I can pray down on each—
       Berkeley's God smiling down from a plane to
Memphis.

My Captain banks hard north now,
       the woman next to me coughs in her sleep,
& light spills onto the arm rest between—warmth
       reminding me whose job is whose 'round here.

III. The Heartlands

"I finally left the furniture store. It was in 1934. My sister, I think, introduced me to a priest. His name was Father Leander Connolly. He used to serve retreat here at St. John's. He stayed awhile and maybe a short time later, maybe a week or two, I don't recall, but she asked me if I would take him to Jacksonville. Now he could have got on the bus and rode to Jacksonville, but he asked me if I would take him. I had an old car at that time. It was a different one, I think it was a 1929.

He was, I think he was Irish. He had a good personality. I asked him, 'Do you know anybody, business or something, where I could get a job?' He said, 'No,' he didn't know anybody. I figured that he'd be well known. We talked about other things and when he got out of the car over at Jacksonville—I took him over there to the hospital—he gave me a rosary. He said, 'Why don't you carry this, maybe you'll get a job.' Well the following Thursday I got my first job where I got paid sixty dollars a month."

—Walter Gardiner, *Memoir*

Blinds Down; Middle of Nowhere

i.m. Walter Gardiner & Gardiner Glass Company

Stashed between the New Madrid fault
And trailer parks preaching Armageddon,
Surveyors all, we claim to measure the pulse
Of the real, pre-Wal-Mart, midwest.

Castaneda's hawks perch on every third
power line staring at Dodge Rams and clear lands.

Three afternoons this week I had different looks
at deer off Chataqua at Reservoir Road—a thick field of them
looking like ostrich next to each other.
Heads down, up, grazing in stubble.

On the shotgun weekend, two came to my gravel drive.
I looked to the woods behind them, saw myself in hunters' sights
caught between the open lands and the front door, stuck
in the backward shadow of my reflected headlights.

These are my people: Missouri guerillas,
master glazers, and marijuana growers.
My family tree washed down the Ohio,
flotsam on the Southern Illinois shore.

Cartographers

"If the ancients believed," as Wyatt might say,
the stars affect us any way,
then, I think, I'd put more stock
in my father's Chrysler radio—

the sky would be late 1960s blue;
he'd be wearing a Munsingwear t-shirt,
Bermuda shorts. Mom would definitely do
her then blond hair up in a scarf.
The red, always red, convertible
would be hurtling down Oak Park Avenue.

I'd be waving little hands and
rocking Snoopy sunglasses to the sky:
tracking all those points, charting angles,
and measuring the scale of that dashboard,
that whitewall, that bungalow, and
the green-lensed sunglasses—

the constellations by which I'd seek return.

Coping Saw

At six I was given a coping saw,
a good thing that a kid couldn't damage
himself with. Balsa wood and two-by-fours
and back basement rafters caught hell from that
toothed skinny, jagged, stretched out blade.

Indian belts; six-shooters; frogs and indy cars
would skate across the dark red linoleum
outside the screen door of his basement shop.

At my parents' on holidays, I see
glimmers in the corners of their kitchen,
brightness in the low pile of the worn rug upstairs.

It's only alone, looking for something
to put all my scraps to right, that I can
watch Dzia Dzia Duda years ago now

knead wood through his jigsaw and make my world
out of pegboard, cast off aluminum, and the orange
light of Shebona Park through his basement windows.

Ode to Buzzy Santos

I never actually met Buzzy Santos.
I think (occasionally) he was our fiction:
A shadow around the corner; tires squealing out
Of the half-lit White Hen at Dixon & Olympus.

He drove by wearing cut-offs on every Honda;
Could buy cases of liquor in any Walgreens;
Ran our neighborhood from the borders of our need
For something to keep us from sleeping early;
Haunted us with a life we could watch
From open garage doors after ten o'clock in August.

Other nights, we'd sneak out to Memorial Park
With three or four beers stolen from McGuire's garage,
Sit at the bottom of twirling slides. Lightning bugs,
Airplane lights, and the flare (we knew) of cigarettes—
His girlfriend's, his own, and somebody's joints—answered
our warm beer musings from the stubble fields where Buzzy stood.

Bitten by suburban nights, mosquitoes,
and some weird insatiable foraging instinct
To explore further into the now and known—
Sidewalks, cul-de-sacs, and new playground equipment—
We were like raccoons knocking over the garbage
Cans of some parents' wish of "what a home should be."

I never really met Buzzy Santos.
But tonight, I know I see him standing
Reflected in the dark window of one
Of those metal-grated store fronts on State Street—
Stereos and cell phones turning
Slow circles on their stands, next to fake furs,
Fake gold, fake foreign stuff from Toledo, OH.

Buzzy's standing out there tonight with one
Hand in somebody else's back pocket,
The other clutching a brick of cordite
Shaped like my small hand ready to blow the
"Oriental Electronic Outlet"
To its place among the half-thoughts of my adolescent
  drives home.

The Rage of Dancing Angels

In the dark, I could just see God in my dad's
half face lit by the hall light over my shoulder.
I would lean young and stupid-drunk in the
open doorway and listen.

Over the heartbeat of my mother's breath,
I could hear him sing or cry in his sleep,
quietly, like the slow turning of cotton sheets.
I could hear clearly, walking into sleep,

for the first time, what it was that I didn't
know that I hadn't done again. As I
spun myself to sleep among the cross-eyed
angels, I understood that the smaller

cherubs sang simply because their God does not dream.

Ode to Paul Desmond

*"My name is Paul Desmond and here I am 30 years old and
this is my first album…"*

You look like my father.
Horn-rimmed early sixties glasses and
a geek cool about your picture that'll fall for back up singers
but shows now only in using words like "former" in your
    liner notes.

I notice your hands though.
Gangly around an alto sax.
Altos are supposed to skylark--dance above the clouds
born in places that've seen nothing but dusty sparrows.

You're looking up at a mike and I know
you don't dance. You have the gift
for being imminently sane, quiet
big-hand articulate when the time is changing around you.

Your liner notes seem as important to you as S.F.S.U.
    workshops where
your Black Panther classmates came armed to class.
    You're understated;
and I imagine you're somewhere re-reading Proust now.
Looking up at a tree with a Clifford Brown stare, precise.

You're listening without headphones to the playback.
The mike's a shadow in a spotlight
I can't imagine you'd step forward into.
Big hands and glasses, waiting through the playback
so the work can begin, seeing it all again, chord over chord.

The Lincoln Trail

There were these sad cellos
playing along I-74 to Springfield.
I've never known a happy cello,
but I know that in our gone family farms
the alarm clock radio in the kitchen
never heard anything sadder than Tommy Dorsey
over the rattle of dishes on Sunday nights.

Hank and his two brothers were in polka band.
Grandpa's banjo was hung up the year Teddy died of TB.
At eight, I found a clarinet behind the storms in the workshed.
Without making a sound, I tasted splinters and dust and told no one.

Old route 36 reminds me of these things.
Just out of radio range, I'm listening between static,
not willing to give up on the cellos or the talk.
The road stretches out along dusty splintered window panes
that I place cobwebs in at 60 m.p.h.
It's almost as if you could play them.
String music that would slowly give way

To winter dances, and wedding dinners, and Grandma--
Platinum blond on another man's arm,
Decades before she'd be brought out here
To be found out, dancing in the kitchen, alone in mid-afternoon.

Second Street Pesach

They sit till sundown on Sunday, quiet
on the front porch in Springfield. Hands folded
in mute conversation and militant piety.

My elder aunt and great grandmother—
displaced catholics, paternal observers
of the Bible belt, the tomb, and cinder streets.

Great grandmother stood six feet tall;
her runaway sister would speak little, at all.
Her silence knew the Kishinev pogrom.
Her husband was still; a picture in the bedroom mirror—
in a prayer shawl, standing in important pose,
obscured by the lacey dress of the Child of Prague.

As the sun went down on Second Street,
they stood, straightened their skirts,
and went in to their next glasses of wine.

They disappear with my crooked memory
past the mezuzah and into the same silence of the day;
the vacuum that all our pasts are becoming.

Glazer Baseball

My grandparents' pine tree grew through the fence;
Without that shade, the garage workshop fell itself.

The backyard became a great green straw mat
whose sticky silence I would shatter
on weekend visits with my whiffle bat,
flailing the air to the backbeat of cracking glass.

Gardiner's Glass Company was a one-
man show. Grandpa's knotty gray knuckles
put up the wooden sign, painted the truck,
penciled and etched each line in stacked, broken sheets of glass

laid over rug-wrapped benches, carpeted
saw horses. Quick taps of the ball-peen.
Precise, lines branching out towards the doorway.
Sundance and soap bubble rainbows, he commanded

onto the back of his truck in measured,
kaleidoscopic, pot-hole defying,
three-on-the-tree order, in the alley
that was our warning track.

My grandparents' pine tree grew through the fence;
Without that shade, the garage workshop fell itself.

A letter to Florence

i.m. Florence Sherwood Gardiner (1917-1994)

They were cleaning out the Temple the morning I heard—
sweeping down cobwebs, folding tables up.
The whole parlor closed, and the quiet consumed me.
That morning I thought of rosary beads and

that mass is only as long as a grandma's rosary.
A given life only so long as our fingers
counting beads, snapping beans, or set squarely
on the round edge of a kitchen table.

That morning's reading said simply to me,
"I am eaten up with zeal for your house" (Jn 2:17).
I know your house simply as another
place, like others, I haven't been enough.

And of all the things that I think I know,
I know so little of you. Only that
cornstarch and flour are mixed for breading,
and when you were a little girl...something....

Your past to me,
despite the genealogy,
is the sandy shore of Tiberias (Jn 21).

Looking east over quiet soybean fields,
back through your four-hundred year old English name,
back through silence like empty interstates
to the creases around your eyes,

I know only:

The zeal for your house consumes me.

Coming Back

I wanted them to be older,
the crossing guard to have gone gray,
and the pavement to have buckled
mercilessly. But it was Indian summer,
hot October, sunny, cruel.

On Ithaca, Eumaios
had the natural decency
to cry for the undead.
There's no decency here;
no Return for a non-hero.

A hero doesn't simply live.
Doesn't as easily follow
the path of yellow or gold leaves
as they fall slowly by themselves;
doesn't walk the dog, stare too long

At six colors in a maple,
or carry his daughter to bed,
asleep, her head rolled soft over
dreaming and alright,
as a non-hero learns from her

to live simply; be heroic.

My last pheasant hunt

I'll follow you a little longer
Through the rough places:
For golden birds do commonly
Vibrate above your head
And pheasants rise at your feet
Wherever you care to walk.

> — Seán Ó Tuama, "Siúlóid in Éirinn"
> Trans. Robert Welch

Out of Lexington, Illinois where old Route 66 meets 55
I'm waiting in maybe the last town without fast food

After driving alongside Joliet, Kankakee, Bloomington—
Brown cities people go home to for Christmas.

These central Illinois fields are hard in December. What
    low sun there is returns to wash
Over the dark soil and leaves the night frost there all day.

I hunted pheasant once in the Nebraska rain and think since
That I can look at all the corn and frozen creek beds differently.

When Grandpa showed up in the car from Springfield,
    I told him
I only got a small game license, but I'm fooling nobody.

He told me he shot at squirrels when he kept chickens
    in the yard,
That eggs were 40 cents a dozen, and his bootlegger uncle
    set up his coop.

He told me that Lexington has a coffee shop that charges $1.45
For coffee and a slice. He told me that he was told
    that he had liver cancer;

That it made him real tired but it wouldn't spread and he
    was proud
That the doctors all knew Mary-Jo. He didn't know why
    I'd listen

To Bill Monroe. Though he told me he liked the Blue Note
    tape I brought
But hadn't heard of Clifford Brown. I never got to tell him
    more about Brown,

Even though Grandpa played saxophone himself before
    he got married.
Later on, he told me that he stopped in the Lexington
    coffee shop and

The pie's bad and he keeps a thermos of coffee in the car,
    when he does drive.
The place is just past the McDonald's that I didn't see.

When we both disappeared up from the downstate fields
    that day,
Flushed from where we came from & without much said
    as usual,

I told him about the last pheasant I saw the morning after
    Thanksgiving—
A hen, outside of Verdon, sprang in a broken arc from
    under my feet

Up from the ground, I traced it down the barrel of the shotgun
As it threw itself in a wide sweep over the broken corn
    along Dry Branch Creek

And back into cover against a cloudy sky, Whisky Run,
And a derelict corn crib while a truck drove south through
    the rain on 75.

That last pheasant showed me toward home. She let us
    know that
We can live in a place where the fields themselves can
    sometimes spare a life.